THE ART
OF MODELING
CHOCOLATE

Published by Goff Books. An Imprint of ORO Editions
Gordon Goff: Publisher

www.goffbooks.com
info@goffbooks.com

Graphic Design: Amanda Pfeifer   Edited by: Ryan Buresh
Production Assistance: Meghan Martin   Translation: Christopher Goff

10 9 8 7 6 5 4 3 2 1 First Edition

Library of Congress data available upon request. World Rights: Available

ISBN: 978-1-939621-21-4

Color Separations and Printing: ORO Group Ltd.
Printed in China.

International Distribution: www.oroeditions.com/distribution

ORO Editions makes a continuous effort to minimize the overall carbon footprint of its publications. As part
of this goal, ORO Editions, in association with Global ReLeaf, arranges to plant trees to replace those used in the
manufacturing of the paper produced for its books. Global ReLeaf is an international campaign run by American
Forests, one of the world's oldest nonprofit conservation organizations. Global ReLeaf is American Forests' education
and action program that helps individuals, organizations, agencies, and corporations improve the local and global
environment by planting and caring for trees.

TABLE OF CONTENTS

4 Introduction

6 Modeling Chocolate

10 A Cake is Born

14 Tools

18 Recipe Corner

24 Basic Techniques

28 Using Color

34 Africa

50 The Americas

68 Antarctica

88 Asia

140 Europe

154 Oceania

168 Acknowledgments

INTRODUCTION

The purpose of this little book is to open up our hidden worlds of fancy and fantasy—to reawaken the child slumbering in us all.

When we played with clay or Play-Doh. When we put together puzzles and built cities from blocks. When we dreamed of fantastic worlds and characters; when nightfall swept us away to new adventures, where we were both the actors and the spectators of our imagination. Back then when we were children, our imaginations overflowed with limitless energy, heedless of the passing time.

Now, as adults, we are often compelled to put our imaginations aside.

This book is dedicated to everyone who would like to return, just for a moment, to the child's world of imagination—who wants to relax, to plunge into a world of fantasy by creating delicious cakes for young and old alike, bringing smiles to their lips and wonder to their dazzled eyes.

MODELING CHOCOLATE

MELT FOR MODELING CHOCOLATE

You may be wondering: what is modeling chocolate?

Modeling chocolate is composed essentially of chocolate (dark, milk, or white) and corn syrup. In Europe, where corn syrup is not widely available, we replace it with water, powdered sugar, and glucose (for elasticity). This mixture is ideal for covering and decorating cakes, cupcakes, and cake pops. Children love it, adults savor it, and you, the dessert artist, will make it your own!

In the cake design world, modeling chocolate is an interesting alternative to fondant (not to everyone's taste) and marzipan (expensive and harder to handle). In addition to these advantages, it is easily sculpted, sturdy, and deliciously chocolaty. Just what a cake designer needs.

Modeling chocolate is easy to work with. Once made it requires no additives, such as water, to stick pieces together—no hours of waiting for them to solidify. It may be dyed the same way as plain fondant. You're the artist—you have free rein to use your instinct for color. The only problem is heat or hot weather. This makes modeling chocolate melt and become greasy, which doesn't help your design work. Handle it no more than necessary and take a break when it starts to get shiny.

Storage is no problem—it keeps as long as a chocolate bar and can be refrigerated. Its expiration date is the same as that of the chocolate used to make it.

Delicious, easily shaped, and universally popular, modeling chocolate has it all—just don't start nibbling before you'e finished your design.

Budding cake designers, here's your recipe!

TIP:
If you're in a hurry and your chocolate is melting, put it in the refrigerator for a few minutes.

RECIPE: MODELING CHOCOLATE

1

2

3

4

5

9

TIP:
No need to struggle with your glucose: warm it in the microwave for a few seconds.

6

7

400 g White or Milk Chocolate (minimum 30% cocoa butter)
105 g Glucose
50 g Powdered Sugar
30 ml Water

For 500 grams of modeling chocolate:
1. Melt 400 g of chocolate in a double boiler.
2. Dissolve 50 g of powdered sugar in 30 mL water.
3. Add 105 g of glucose.
4. Mix into a smooth syrup.
5. Add this syrup to the chocolate and mix until the paste comes together and stops clinging to the sides of the bowl.
6. Let it cool for a few minutes.
7. Wrap the fondant in plastic film and let it rest at least 12 hours (ideally 48 hours) at room temperature.

Corn Syrup Option:
165 g of Corn Syrup
400 g of Milk or White Chocolate (minimum of 30% cocoa butter)

1. Heat your corn syrup and melt your chocolate.
2. Pour corn syrup into melted chocolate and mix until the paste comes together and stops clinging to the sides of the bowl. Try not to overmix.
3. Let it cool and wrap it.

A CAKE IS BORN

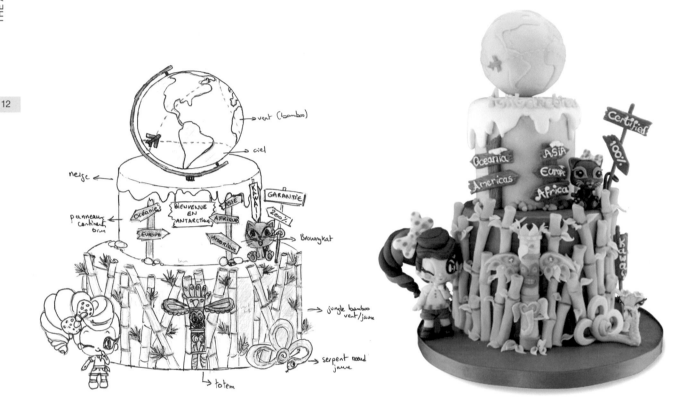

Our ideas, our colors, our dreams, all begin with our imagination and our personal experience. If you're like me—overflowing with creativity— do take every opportunity to draw whatever inspires you, at any time of the day or night (when our imagination is anything but drowsy). This will allow you to visualize the end result, position the elements to be sculpted, and ensure a beautiful color scheme. Don't worry, you don't have to be Picasso or Dali (as far as I know, neither dabbled in cake design!)—the point is simply to bring your ideas into focus when you have them and avoid wasting time.

If it's a struggle to feel creative, don't hesitate to riffle through your library or surf the web for inspriation. Books and the internet are a goldmine when you're prospecting for that shining creative nugget!

TOOLS

1. Mini Cutters
2. Brushes, Scalpel, and Clay Shaper Brush
3. Round Cutters

4. Piping Nozzles
5. Cutters
6. Silicone Rolling Pin

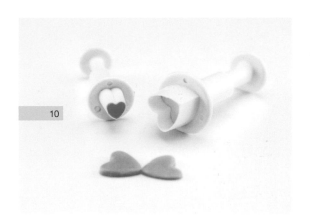

7. Food Coloring
8. Sugar Gun
9. Plunger Cutters

10. More Plunger Cutters
11. Mini Plunger Cutters
12. Modeling Tool Kit: large/small veining tool, shell tool/knife, large/small dogbone tool, serrated quilting/cutting wheel, umbrella tool with 5 & 6 divisions, scriber/cone tool, large/small ball tool, palette knife, modeling sticks #1 & #2

RECIPE CORNER

CHOCOLATE CAKE

Ingredients

200 g Dark Chocolate
180 g Confectioner's Sugar
100 g Flour
½ Envelope Baking Powder [approx. 7-11 g]
75 g Butter
5 Eggs, separated

Serves 8 people | Preparation Time: 10 minutes | Baking Time: 45 minutes (180°C)

Preheat oven to 180°.

1. Break 200 g dark chocolate into pieces; melt with butter in a double boiler.
2. Remove from heat and stir in 180 g of sugar.
3. Add egg yolks.
4. Sift flour and baking powder together; add to chocolate mixture.
5. Beat egg whites until stiff and gently fold into chocolate mixture.
6. Pour into a buttered, parchment-lined cake pan.

Bake approximately 45 minutes at 180°C (convection oven). Wrap the cake immediately to keep it moist and tender inside and out.

SUGGESTION:
Even better made a day ahead!

VEGAN CHOCOLATE CAKE

Ingredients

125 g Whole Wheat Pastry Flour or Unbleached
All-Purpose Flour
150 g Vanilla Sugar or Sugar Cane
50 g Dark Vegan Chocolate
5 g Baking Powder
2-3 Spoonfuls Unsweetened Cocoa Powder
1/5 tspn Salt
175 mL Soya Vanilla Milk or Chocolate
Vanilla Milk
80 mL Unsweetened Applesauce
40 mL Vegetable Oil
1 tspn Pure Vanilla Extract

Preheat oven to 180°.

1. Mix the vanilla or chocolate Soya milk,
vegetable oil, vanilla extract and applesauce in a
large mixing bowl.
2. Beat until foamy.
3. In another bowl, mix flour, sugar, cocoa
powder, and salt. Slowly sift over the wet
ingredients while mixing with a hand-held of
standing mixer.
4. Melt the dark chocolate and pour into your
batter. It should be creamy and pourable.
5. Pour batter in your cake pan.

Bake 45-50 minutes, or until a toothpick inserted
into the center comes out clean. Let cool
completely before frosting.

CHOCOLATE MASCARPONE GANACHE

Ingredients

100 g Dark Chocolate

125 g Mascarpone

3 tblspn Powdered Sugar

Preparation

1. Break 100 g dark chocolate into pieces. Melt in a double boiler.

2. Remove from heat. Mix in mascarpone and powdered sugar.

CHOCOLATE HONEY CREAM GANACHE

Ingredients

125 g Dark Chocolate

125 g Heavy Cream (or vegan Soya Cream)

50 g Butter (or vegan Soya Margarine)

40 g Honey

Preparation

1. Break 125 g dark chocolate into pieces. Melt with butter in a double boiler.

2. Remove from heat. Mix in honey and cream.

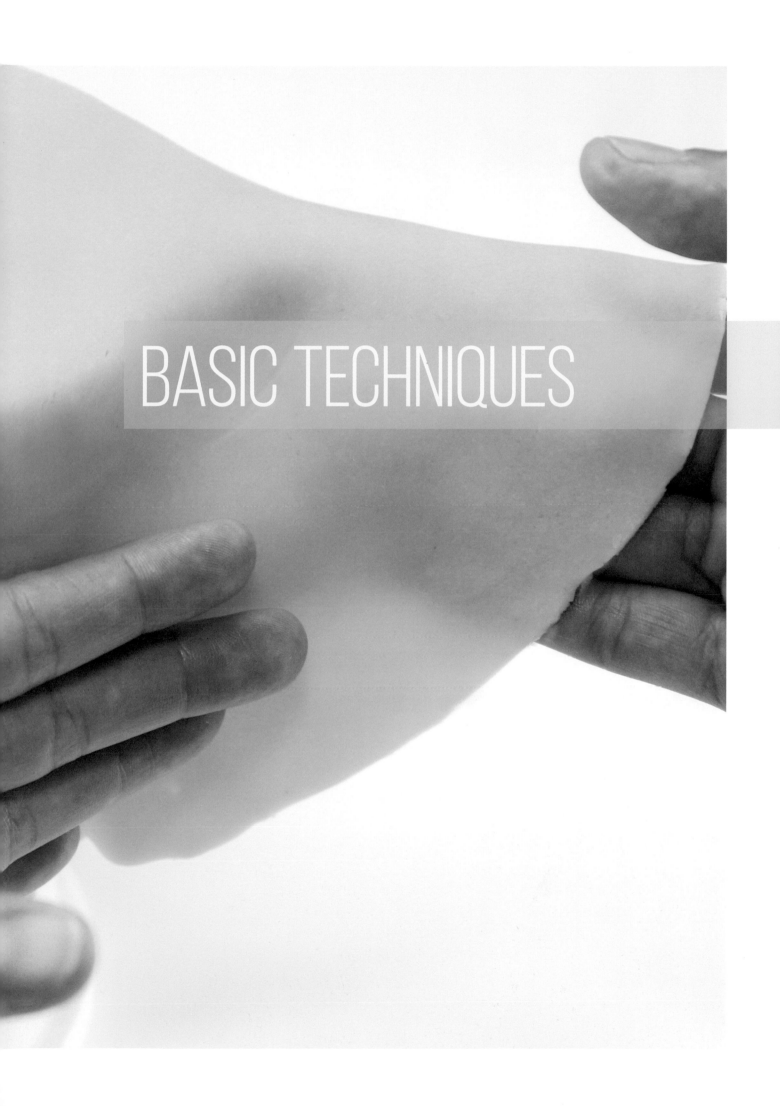

BASIC TECHNIQUES

FILLING A CAKE

1. Cut your cake into 3 or more layers of equal thickness. Cover each layer with ganache or other filling. Assemble: then level off the top.

2. Apply ganache to the sides of the assembeled layers and smooth it out.

3. Put a cardboard or acrylic disc of the same diameter as the bottom of your cake pan on the top and underneath the cake.

4. Hold a spatula firmly against your revolving cake stand and the disc at a 90° right angle. Apply ganache, scraping off the excess with the spatula. Let harden in the refrigerator for a few minutes.

5. Carefully remove the top disc. Put a little ganache on top.

6. Spread ganache and even out, turning the cake on its axis. Put in the refrigerator for half hour before covering with modeling chocolate.

SUGGESTION:

Put your filled cake in the refrigerator for a half hour before covering it with modeling chocolate.

TIP:

A revolving cake stand makes cake filling and decoration easy.

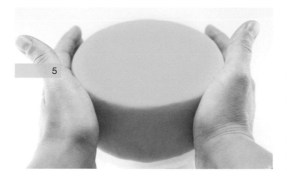

HOW TO COVER A CAKE WITH MODELING CHOCOLATE

1. Roll modeling chocolate thin.
2. Place it on the cake.
3. Hold the skirt of chocolate with one hand and with the other press up and in. Be careful not to touch the fragile upper edge; you may break it. Always start at the center and work towards the bottom.
4. Use scalpel to remove excess chocolate.
5. Smooth edges carefully for a flawless surface.

TIP:
Use a pot of smaller diameter than the cake as a base. It will make covering the cake with chocolate much easier.

USING COLORS

One of the key elements of cake design is the use of colors.

Understanding the color wheel will ensure a beautiful chromatic composition. You can combine both diametrically opposed and complementary colors. Food coloring provides your palette for cake design. It comes in different forms: gel, powder, paste, even liquid. The latter is to be avoided, for it will alter the texture of your modeling chocolate.

A limitless rainbow may be produced from the three "primary" colors (blue, red, and yellow). When you combine primary colors, you get "secondary" colors (orange, green, and violet). When primary and secondary colors are combined, you get new shades known as "tertiary" colors (yellow-orange, red-orange, reddish violet, violet blue, greenish yellow, and so forth). To get lighter colors, just add white chocolate.

Express yourself through this infinite color variety.

THE COLOR WHEEL

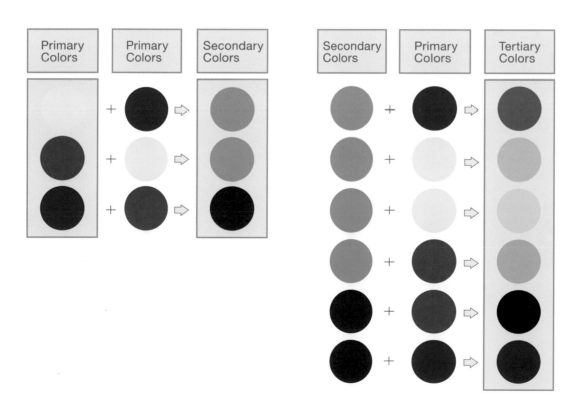

Primary Colors		Primary Colors		Secondary Colors
●	+	●	⇨	●
●	+	●	⇨	●
●	+	●	⇨	●

Secondary Colors		Primary Colors		Tertiary Colors
●	+	●	⇨	●
●	+	●	⇨	●
●	+	●	⇨	●
●	+	●	⇨	●
●	+	●	⇨	●
●	+	●	⇨	●

HOW TO COLOR A CAKE

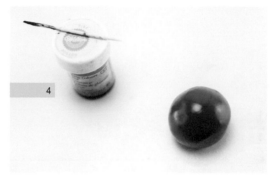

Materials
Gel Colors
Disposable Gloves, non-powdered
Toothpicks
Modeling Chocolate

1. Dip the toothpick in gel color. Apply to chocolate.
2. Put on disposable plastic gloves and knead color in.
3. If necessary, add another dab of color to acheive desired hue.

SUGGESTION:
Color your chocolate the day before decorating
to save time on Design Day.

AFRICA

LION

MASK DECORATIONS

1. Make three balls, each of a different color and roll out.
2. Cut out using a round cutter.
3. Make a leaf shape.
4. Cut leaves of different sizes and colors and place them one on top of the other. Cut black hearts for noses.
5. Round off the top of the masks.
6. For the Giraffe, cut the base in a semi-circle.

GIRAFFE

7. Cut off the top of a black heart.
8. Roll out brown modeling chocolate and cut out a bunch of tiny flowers, one next to the other, to make lace.
9. Position it on the ebony mask and smooth down.
10. Use a teardrop plunger cutter to hollow out the eyes. Make the nostrils.

ZEBRA

11. Cut out several thin strips.
12. Use a heart-shaped cutter to cut off the bottom of the mask.
13. Inset the black heart shape for the nose. Draw the nostrils. Hollow the eyes and attach the ears.
14. Add the zebra stripes to the mask.

ANTELOPE

15. Make a thin ribbon using your sugar gun. Twist the tips to make horns.
16. Place horns on the antelope mask. Make eyes, ears, nose, etc., as before.

LION'S BODY

17. Make a 25 g ball, then mold it to a pear shape using the palm of your hand.
18. Cut off the tip.
19. Roll a 24 g sausage shape and cut it into four.
20. Use a rolling pin to flatten one end of each piece.
21. Mark off the foot using your brush shaper.
22. Smooth with your ring finger.
23. Bend the foot.
24. Form four 1/8 g white balls each and flatten it on one edge.
25. Put it on the underside of the paw.
26. Use your leaf tool to draw toes.
27. Mark off the knee.
28. Pinch the back.
29. Position the rear legs.
30. Smooth out joins.

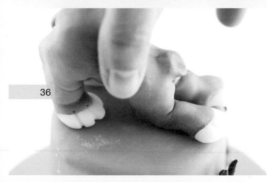

31. Repeat Steps 29 and 30.

32. Fold the front legs 90°.

33. Flatten the paw slightly.

34. Position the front legs and smooth out joins.

35. Stick a toothpick in the underside of each rear leg to attach it to the cake.

36. Position the body on the cake.

37. Stick another toothpick in the neck, in between the legs.

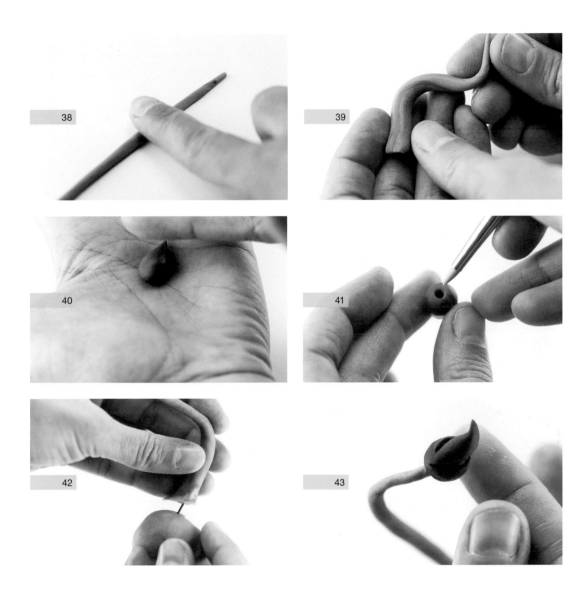

TAIL

38. Roll a thin piece with one end thicker than the other.
39. Give it curves.
40. Form a bulb shape.
41. Make a hole.
42. Position tail and smooth out joins.
43. Place the end tuft of the tail.

FUR

44. Make a 9 g teardrop, flatten the base.

45. Using your leaf tool, making slanting strokes all around.

46. Pinch here and there to create tufts.

47. Insert a toothpick and arrange fur around the neck.

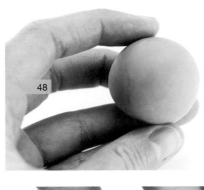
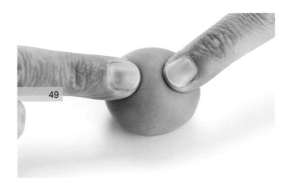

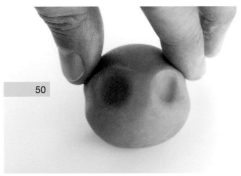

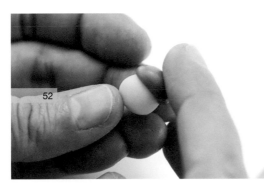

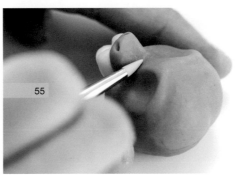

HEAD

48. Make a 30 g ball.
49. Using your index finger, shape the eye sockets.
50. Pinch to shape muzzle.
51. Make two spheres, one brown, one white. Cut the brown sphere in half.
52. Position one of the halves onto the white sphere.
53. Make a slanting cut for the mouth and shape the nostrils.
54. Push in the small bone modeling tool and pull down. Round out the lower jaw if necessary.
55. Position the muzzle and smooth out joins.

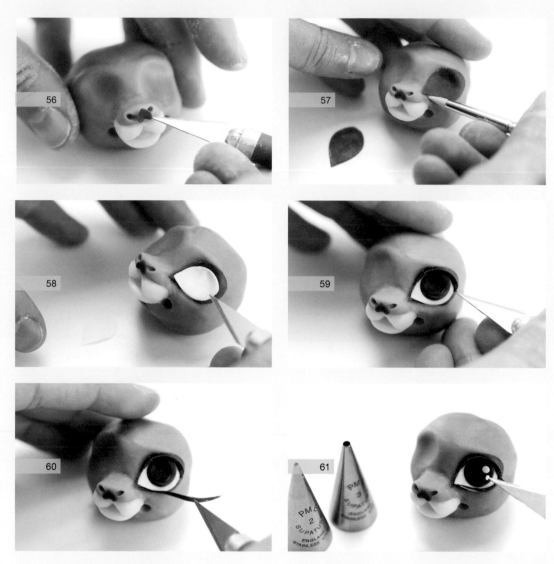

56. Cut out a heart for the nose.

EYES

57. Cut two teardrop shapes. Position them on the eye sockets.

58. Cut a white teardrop for the eye.

59. Cut out two circles, a brown for the retina and a black one for the pupil. Reduce the pupil. Place a thread for the lashes.

60. Arrange the lashes around the white teardrop and remove excess.

61. Cut out two circles with piping nozzles 2 and 3 for highlights.

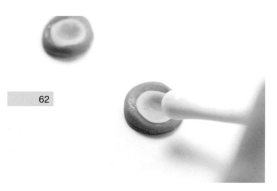

EARS

62. Make a ball, cut it in two, flatten it, and use the small bone modeling tool to make a hollow shape.

63. Use a rounded cutter to remove part of the base.

64. Position the ears. Smooth out and blend the joins.

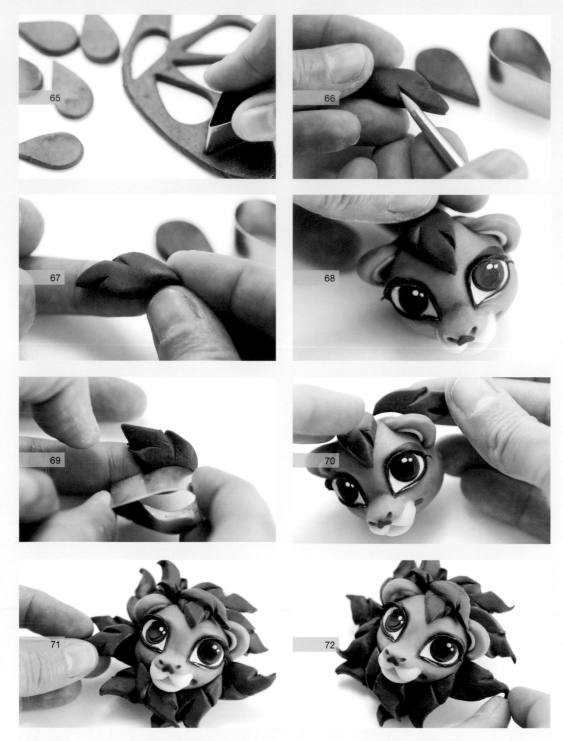

MANE

65. Roll brown modeling chocolate 2mm thick and cut out a dozen teardrop shapes.

66. Using your leaf tool, make slanting strokes all around the center.

67. Using your teardrop cutter, cut a piece off a teardrop shape.

68. Position the forelock.

69. Using your teardrop cutter, cut a piece off a teardrop shape.

70. Position it behind the ears. Repeat as necessary.

71. Arrange shapes on either side symmetrically.

72. Give shape to the mane.

73. Cut out two dark brown arches.

MOUTH

74. Cut out a pink heart and remove the point. Put it inside the mouth.

75. Make two tiny white cones and position them in the lower jaw.

76. Position the head.

77. Make several tiny white cones and position them in the holes of the feet.

THE AMERICAS

ALLIGATOR

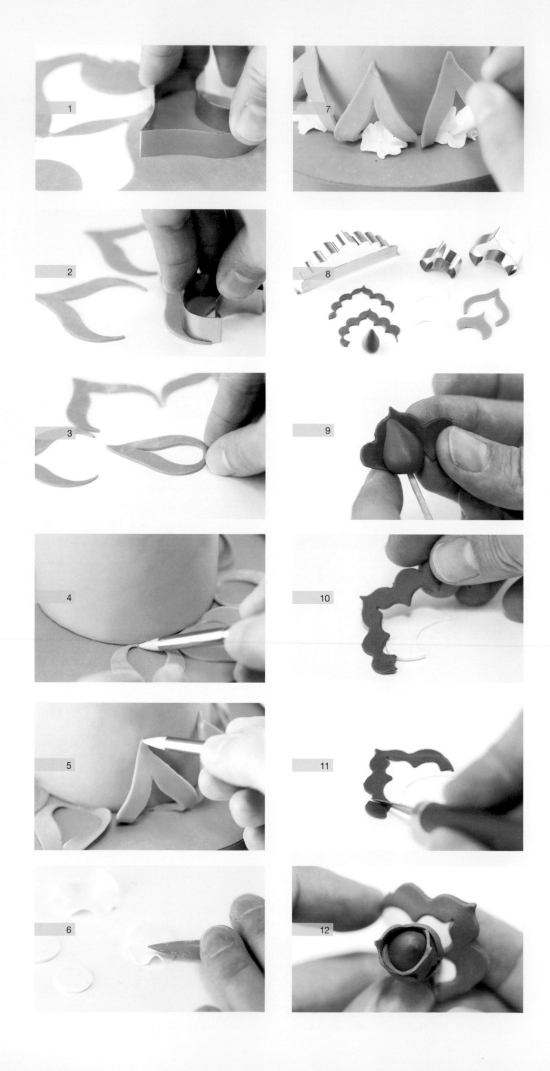

FOLIAGE DECORATION

1. Roll out turquoise modeling chocolate and cut leaf shapes.
2. Recut the leaves to produce arches.
3. Join the ends.
4. Position them all around the cake.
5. Lift and attach points.
6. Cut flowers and ruffle their edges.
7. Position them between arches all around the cake.

FLOWER DECORATION

8. Cut out several pink Mughal arches, white petals, and green arches.
9. Make a bulb shape and arrange overlapping pink petals around it.
10. Arrange pink Mughal arches around the edges of white petals.
11. Cut to even ends out.
12. Add the two-color petals to the flower.

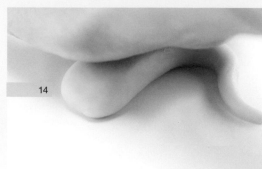

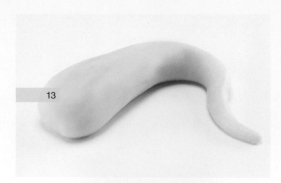

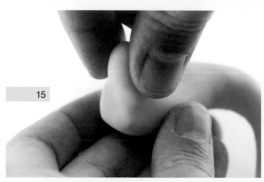

ALLIGATOR'S BODY

13. Make a sausage shape and thin out one end.

14. Flatten slightly.

15. Pull a bit up out of the thicker end.

16. Shape the neck; trim excess.

17. Using leaf tools, mark vertical lines.

18. Add horizontal lines.

19. Mix color and water, paint scales slightly darker.

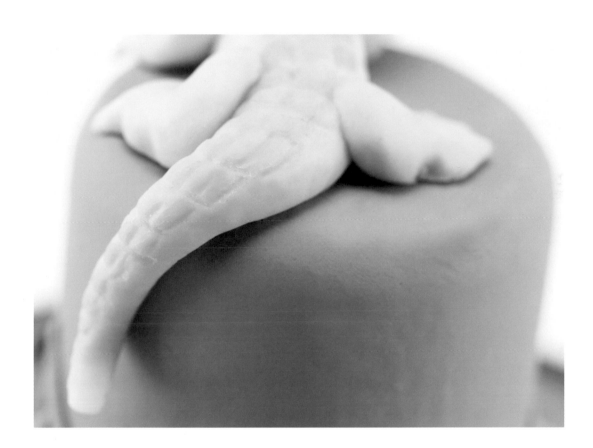

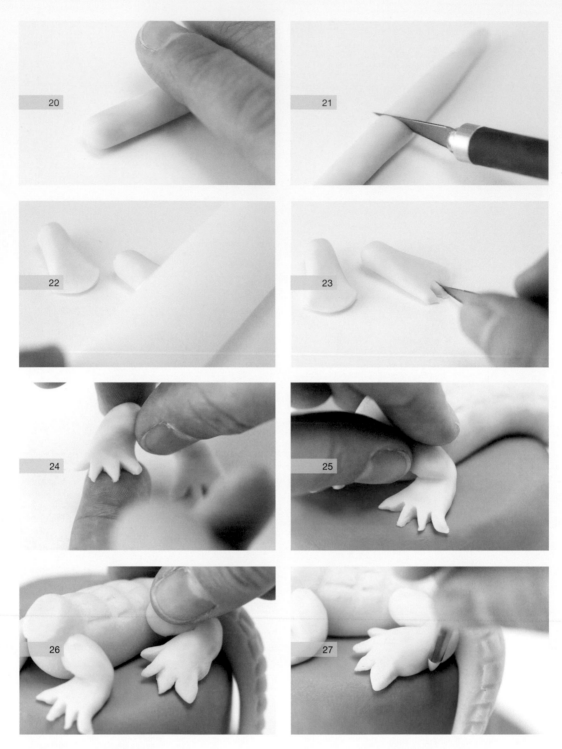

20. Roll a sausage shape.

21. Cut it into four pieces.

22. Flatten one end.

23. Cut out claws.

24. Bend to suggest movement.

25. Position front and back claws.

26. Press firmly onto the alligator's body.

27. Shape folds.

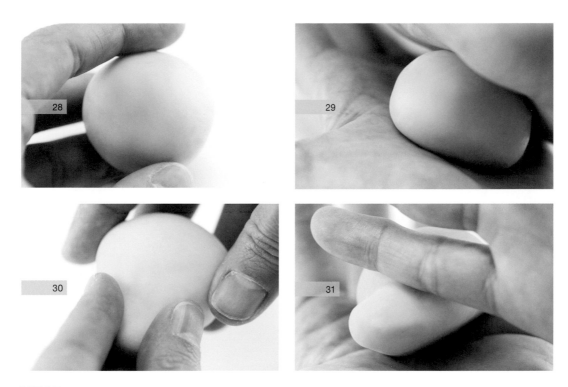

HEAD

28. Make a ball.
29. Flatten it.
30. Pull out and shape muzzle.
31. Using your ring finger, shape the lower jaw and cheeks.

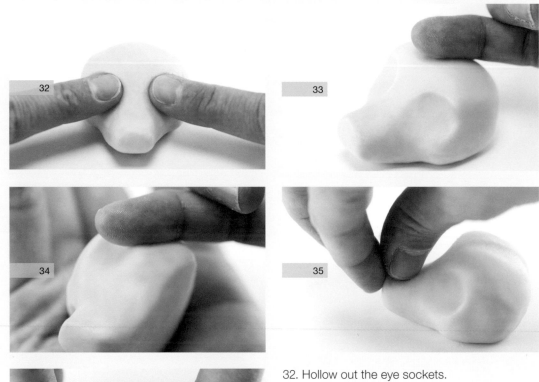

32. Hollow out the eye sockets.
33. Shape the top of the head.
34. And the cheeks.
35. Pinch and pull the muzzle tip slightly upward.
36. Model the temples.

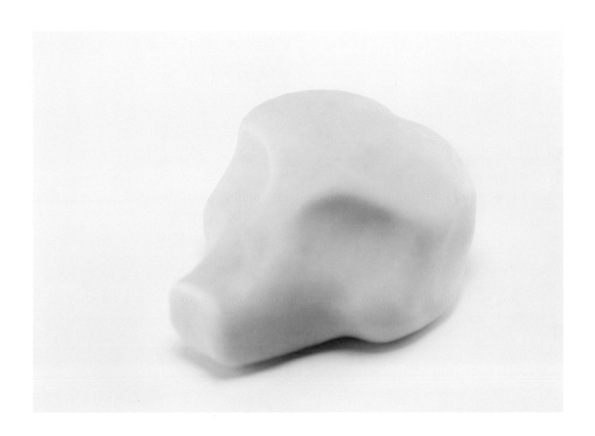

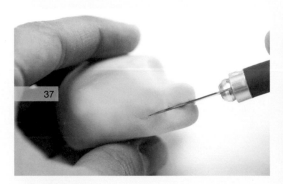

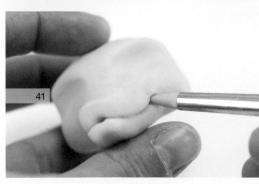

MUZZLE

37. Cut the mouth opening.

38. Push in small bone modeling tool and pivot downwards.

39. Shape the lower jaw.

40. Pinch each corner of the lower jaw.

41. Shape the dimples.

42. Indicate nostrils.

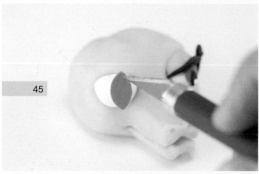

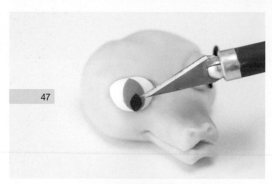

EYES

43. Make a white ball; cut out three progressively smaller leaf shapes for eyelashes, eyelid, and iris, two mini-hearts for the eyelashes, and a teardrop for the pupil.

44. Cut the ball in two; place halves in eye sockets.

45. Apply iris.

46. Take the black teardrop and pinch the bottom.

47. Position the pupil.

48. Position the eyelid on edge.

49. Smooth out joins.

50. Take the black leaf shape and cut out a slightly off-center leaf shape.

51. Position the eyelashes.

52. Trim excess.

53. Add a white highlight.

54. Cut one mini-heart in half.

55. Position one heart and one half-heart on each eye.

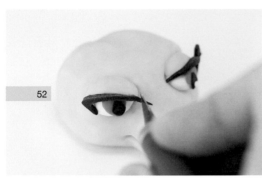

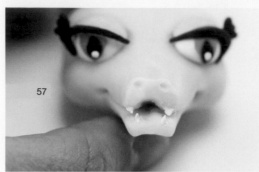

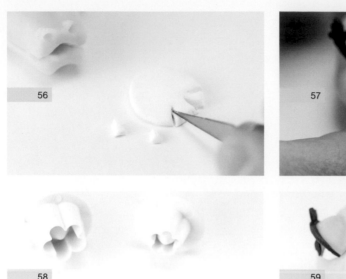

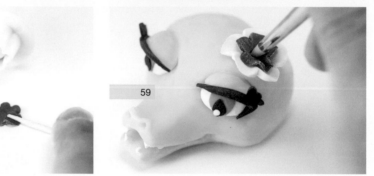

TEETH AND ACCESSORIES

56. Cut out four white mini-cones.

57. Position them in the mouth.

58. Cut out two flowers and ruffle their edges.

59. Put them on the head.

60. Finally, shape the muzzle folds and paint a tone darker.

ANTARCTICA

PENGUIN

SNOW DECORATIONS

1. Roll white modeling chocolate 6mm thick. Cut out snow drips.

2. Smooth edges with bone modeling tool.

3. Round off edges.

4. Shape hollows.

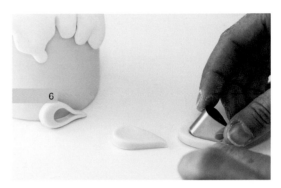

BOW DECORATIONS

5. Cut out three teardrop shapes.

6. Cut out a smaller teardrop shape from each center.

7. Arrange them in a fan.

8. Cut out a circle and a snowflake to finish off the bow.

SNOWFLAKE DECORATIONS

9. Make thin ribbons using your sugar gun.

10. Cut five pieces, each 6cm long, and shape each into a heart.

11. Arrange hearts to form a circle, wide part towards the center.

12. Cut 10 pieces, each 7cm long, and curl the ends in a 'S' shape.

13. Attach each to the point of a heart.

14. Cut five pieces, each 5cm long, and roll. Pinch at either side to make leaf shapes.

15. Arrange the snowflake on your cake and put the leaves at the end of the branches.

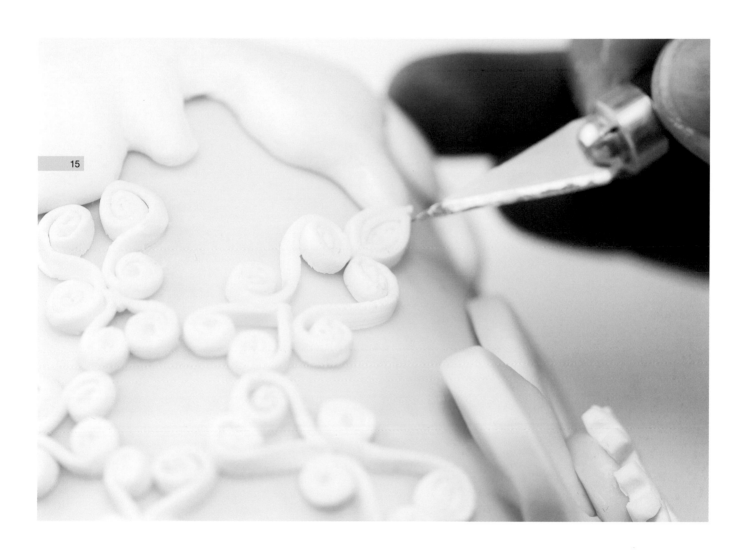

PENGUIN'S BODY

16. Make a ball.

17. Flatten and roll it, using the side of your hand.

18. You should end up with a pear shape.

19. Cut out a teardrop.

20. Position it on the stomach.

21. Cut out two 5-petalled flowers.

22. Mold two petals together to make feet.

23. Put them on the bottom.

WINGS

24. Cut out two teardrops.
25. Flatten the base only.
26. Recut the teardrop and trim excess.
27. This should produce wings thinner at the shoulders.
28. Position the wings.
29. Curl the pointed tips slightly upward.

HEAD

30. Make a ball.
31. Shape the eye sockets.
32. Flatten the head slightly.
33. Shape cheeks with your ring finger.

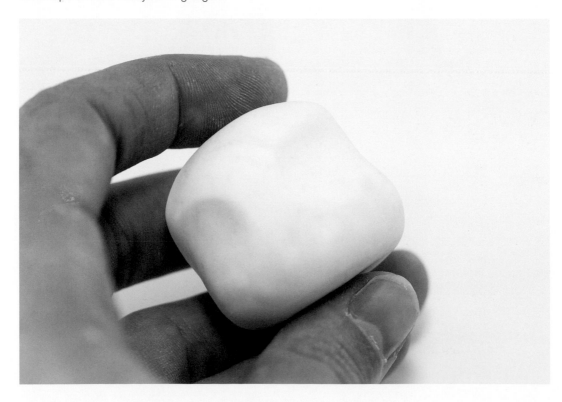

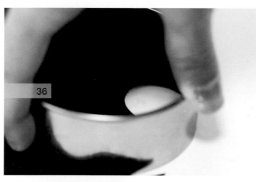

34. Roll out black modeling chocolate and cut two circles.

35. Shorten the nose piece by a few millimeters.

36. Take a round cutter three times as large as the first and cut a circle around the small circles you made earlier.

37. This should give you the penguin's black mask.

38. Position it on the head.

39. Spread very gently to cover the whole head.

40. Shape the top of the head.

41. Now you're ready to add features.

EYES

42. Use cutters to make two flowers, two teardrops, two circles, and two mini-flowers.

43. Use a clay-shaper to ruffle the edges of the larger flowers.

44. Reduce the size of your teardrop.

45. Position it on the flower.

46. Place the circle as the pupil.

47. Cut the assembled eye to show the cure of the cheek.

48. Position the highlights.

49. Repeat for the other eye.

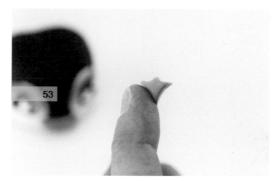

BEAK

50. Cut two little triangles.

51. Round off the points and flatten.

52. Take one triangle and pinch the middle of one side.

53. You should get this.

54. Put it on top of the other part of the beak and mark the dimples.

55. Be sure to add nostrils.

56. Stick a toothpick in the neck.
57. Position the head.
58. Place the mother penguin on the cake.

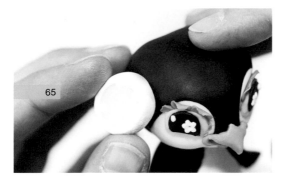

WINTER ACCESSORIES

59. Roll out a little modeling chocolate.

60. Pick a design and place tiny white balls on it to make polka dots.

61. Roll smooth.

62. Cut out two circles.

63. Roll out white modeling chocolate. Cut out two white circles larger than the polka dot circles; cut out their centers, using the same cutter you used for the polka dot circles.

64. Insert polka dot circles into white circles.

65. Place earmuffs on head.

66. Prick the white surface evenly to create texture of the earmuff.

67. Cut a wide ribbon a position it.

SCARF

68. Cut out a long blue ribbon. Position dots.

69. Roll to smooth.

70. Drape carefully around neck; make fringe on either end.

CAP

71. Take two different-sized round cutters. Cut out a white ring. Then a blue circle. Press your finger into the underside of the blue circle to raise it slightly in the middle. Pinch the upper side and pull it into a point. Fold it over. Roll a little ball and put it at the end of the cap. Position the white ring around the edge. Use a toothpick to prick the white parts evenly, giving them texture, and finish with a sprinkle of white edible glitter if you would like.

ASIA

ELEPHANT

CAKE DECORATION

1. Use cutters to produce India-inspired shapes: petals, circles, and teardrops. Cut smaller petals out of your petal shapes, producing arcs. Use them in a decorative frieze.

2. Cut out paisley shapes, petals, dots, and teardrops of various sizes and arrange them as you please. Make lace by using the tip of a pastry tube to punch out teardrops or circles.

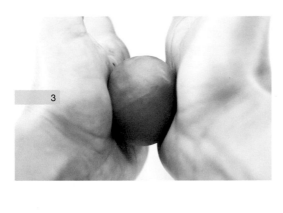

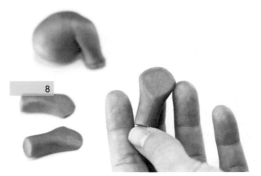

ELEPHANT'S BODY

3. Make a ball smaller than that of the head and flatten it slightly between your hands.

4. Form it into an egg shape.

5. Roll a sausage shape.

6. Cut it into four equal parts.

7. Put each of the four sausages on end and flatten slightly to make a shoulder or thigh.

8. You will get this.

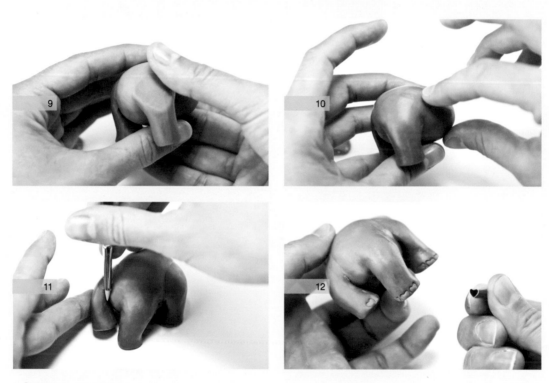

9. Attach to the body.

10. Dip your index finger in water and use it to smooth the joins.

11. Trace wrinkles with your clay-shaper.

12. Use a heart-shaped punch to mark the nails.

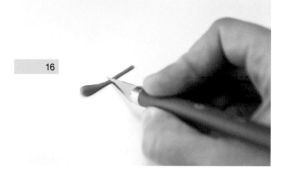

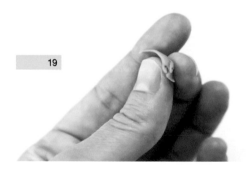

13. Draw the knees.
14. Roll a little ball for the tail.
15. Narrow one end.
16. Cut off the excess.
17. Pinch the other end.
18. Make two lateral cuts.
19. Fold them over.
20. Attach the tail and smooth out the join.

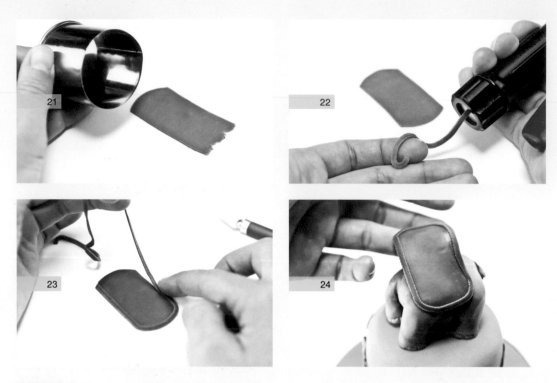

CARPET

21. Cut out a pink strip and, using a round cutter, round off the ends.

22. Put a small ribbon nozzle on your sugar gun.

23. Run a ribbon all around your rectangle.

24. Put the carpet on the elephant's back. Add your own design to the carpet: flowers, paisley shapes, and embroidery.

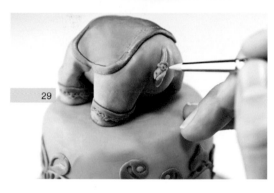
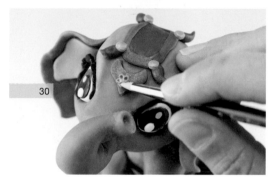

BRACELETS AND ORNAMENTS

25. Cut out four narrow mauve strips and pink flowers.
Cut up the flowers, leaving only three petals.

26. Put them around the feet.

27. Put the ribbon above the flowers.

28. Draw a dot on each petal.

29. Repeat for the elephant's tail.

30. Repeat for the headdress.

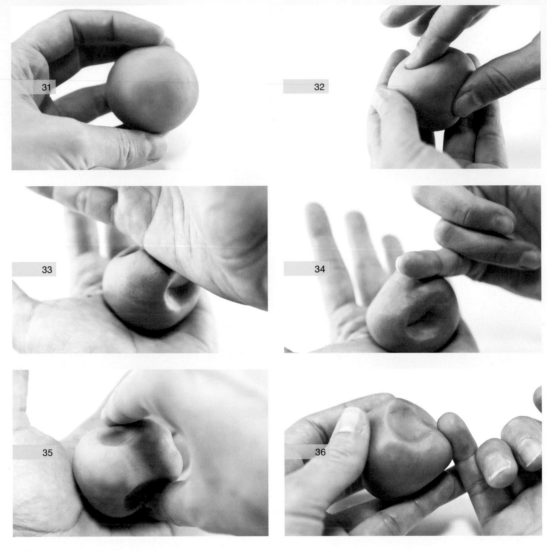

HEAD

31. Make a ball.
32. Using your thumb and index finger, shape the eye sockets.
33. Indent the upper forehead slightly.
34. Use your ring finger to shape the top of the head.
35. Press in slightly at the sides where the ears will go.
36. Draw the cheeks.

EYES

37. Cut out a white circle, a smaller mauve circle for the iris, and an even smaller black circle for the pupil. Cut out two white dots, one large and one small, to give the eyes sparkle. Using a fluter cutter, cut out a fluted arch.

38. Position the iris, the pupil, and the white highlights.

39. Add eyelashes.

40. Suggestion: Add more black dots to emphasize the outer edge of the eye.

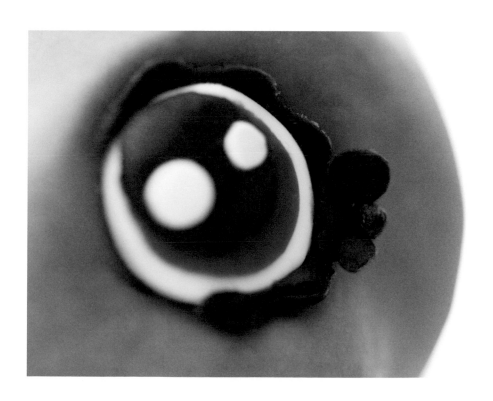

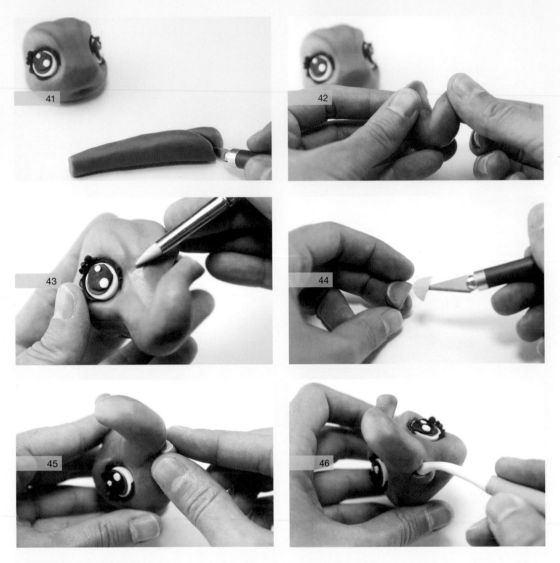

TRUNK AND MOUTH

41. Roll a sausage shape for the elephant's trunk. Narrow one end. Cut the thick end a base.

42. Twist the trunk slightly and make a hollow at the thin end.

43. Position the trunk and smooth the join with water.

44. Cut a mauve teardrop shape for the mouth and a smaller pink one for the tongue.

45. Cut their points off and position them underneath the trunk.

46. Using the bone-modeling tool, hollow and round out the mouth.

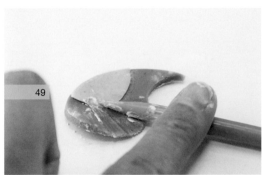

EARS

47. Cut out two teardrop shapes, one mauve, and a smaller pink one.

48. Cut the pink teardrop into an eyeshape.

49. Dust the edge of the outer ear with cornstarch and thin it with a pointed or ball tool.

50. Position the ears.

51. You may now position the head on the body and give the ears the desired effect of movement.

PANDA AND MEI

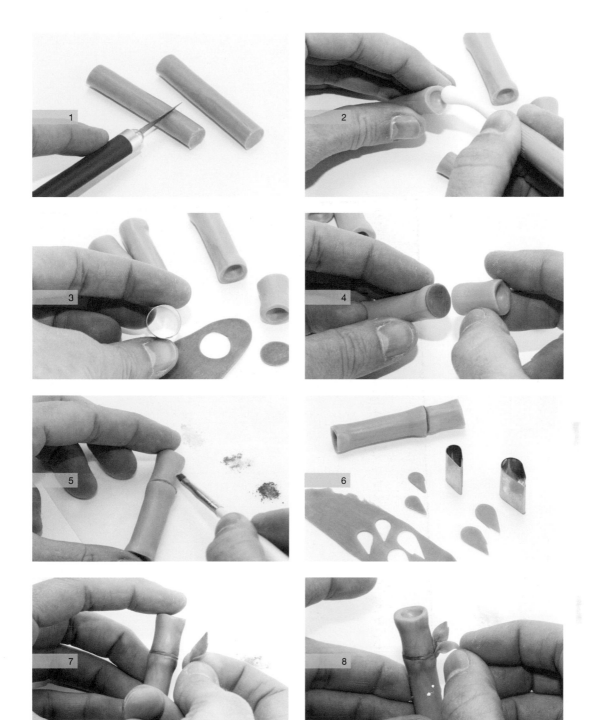

BAMBOO STALKS

1. Take 20 g of modeling chocolate, roll into a sausage shape, and divide into two equal parts each 7 cm long. Cut off a third of each.

2. Using your bone-modeling tool, push in both ends of each piece.

3. Roll a little brown modeling chocolate 1 mm thick and cut out two circles.

4. Sandwich the circle between the two pieces of bamboo.

5. Paint your bamboo and its join vertically with a little yellow and green powdered color. Begin with yellow, then add a shading from light to dark green.

6. Roll a little green modeling chocolate 1 mm thick and cut out a few teardrops of different sizes.

7. Color the center of the leaves in dark green and fold them at the base before placing them on your bamboo stalk.

8. Add another small leaf.

PANDA

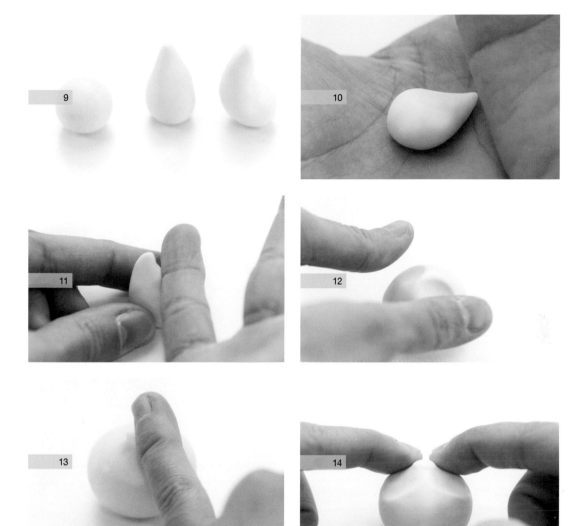

BODY AND HEAD

9. Take 15 g of white modeling chocolate. Make a ball.

10. Shape the ball into a pear.

11. Using your little finger or a brush, indent the hollow of the back.

12. Take 25 g of white modeling chocolate and make a ball. Use your thumbs to hollow the eye sockets.

13. Slightly flatten the area between the eyes.

14. Turn the head upside down and, with your fingers inverted, create the muzzle.

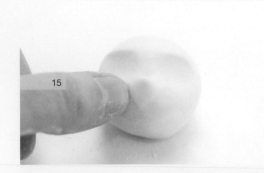

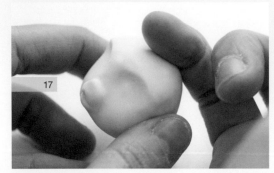

HEAD

15. Contour the muzzle further.

16. Mark the mouth with your clay-shaper.

17. Shape the top of the head, pressing lightly.

18. With the tip of your brush, trace the brow line.

19. Blend away tool marks with your finger.

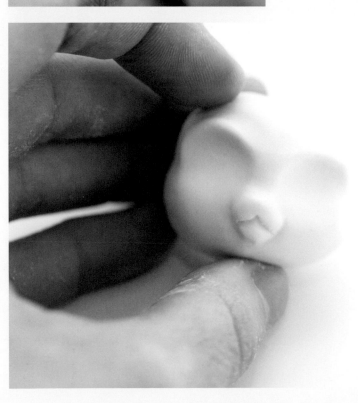

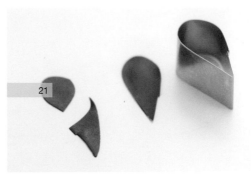

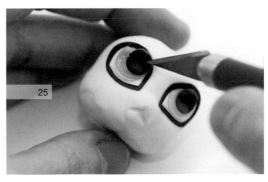

EYES

20. You'll need the following tools: teardrop cutter, pastry tube nozzles N°s 2 and 4, small round cutter, and a small heart-shaped punch cutter.

21. Cut out two black teardrops. Trim them down.

22. Cut out white teardrops. Trim them down.

23. Position the black drop, then the white.

24. Position a small blue drop and trim.

25. Cut out two black circles for the pupils.

26. Cut a tiny heart and position it upside down on the muzzle.

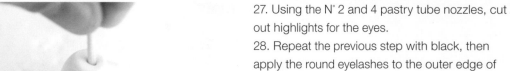

27. Using the Nº 2 and 4 pastry tube nozzles, cut out highlights for the eyes.

28. Repeat the previous step with black, then apply the round eyelashes to the outer edge of each eye.

29. Make a little indentation on either side of the mouth.

30. Use a round cutter to make two circles about 2-3mm thick. Using your small bone-modeling tool, make a hollow in each.

31. Use the round cutter to remove a little from the edge so the ear fits the curve of the head.

32. Postion the ears.

33. Insert a toothpick in the body.

ASSEMBLAGE

34. Position the head.

35. Take a little black modeling chocolate form a small teardrop.

36. Cut down the sides.

37. Position the tail.

38. Take 3 g of black modeling chocolate, roll, and narrow down the middle.

39. Cut.

40. Bend the paw forward.

41. Push the bone-modeling slightly into the paw.

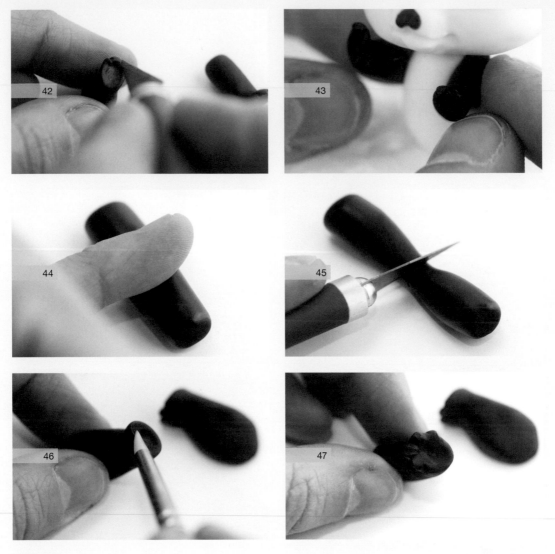

PAWS

42. Model the paws.

43. Position the front paws.

44. Repeat steps 38 with 10 g of modeling chocolate.

45. Repeat step 39.

46. Model the paw again.

47. You will end up with this.

48. Position the paws.
49. Cut out a small pink teardrop for the tongue and position it.
50. Cut two leaves of different sizes and position them on the head.
51. Take pastry tube nozzle N°2, cut out three white dots and a white heart, and position them.
52. Finally, apply a little pink blush to the cheeks.

CAKE DECORATION

1. Take your cake platter and cover it with a thin layer of chocolate. Then roll out your green modeling chocolate less than 1mm thick; cut out little circles. Position them symmetrically.

2. Use your rolling pin gently and evenly to unify the design without distorting the circles.

3. Roll out your mauve modeling chocolate no more than 2mm thick. Cut out a rectangle to cover your cupcake. Then cut a circle with fluted edges. Take round cutter with a diameter 1cm less than that of the fluted circle. Cut out the center of the fluted circle.

4. Cut and turn it into a ribbon.

5. First wrap your rectangle around the cupcake. Then add the fluted ribbon. Smooth away the joins with the clay shaper.

6. Take a little stick and make perpendicular indentations all around the cupcake.

7. Place the cupcake on the board. Then use your sugar gun to make a long green ribbon. Tie it around the cupcake.

8. Fold it into a bow.

9. Roll modeling chocolate 3 to 4mm thick and trace a circle. Cut "drips" all around the circle, being careful not to go inside its diameter.

10. As shown above.

11. Put the "poured" design on top of your cake.

12. Add a few additional drops, smoothing out the joins with your clay shaper.

13. Position the bamboo you made earlier (steps 1-8).

14. Add your little panda (steps 9-46).

15. Put a little bamboo between the panda's paws.

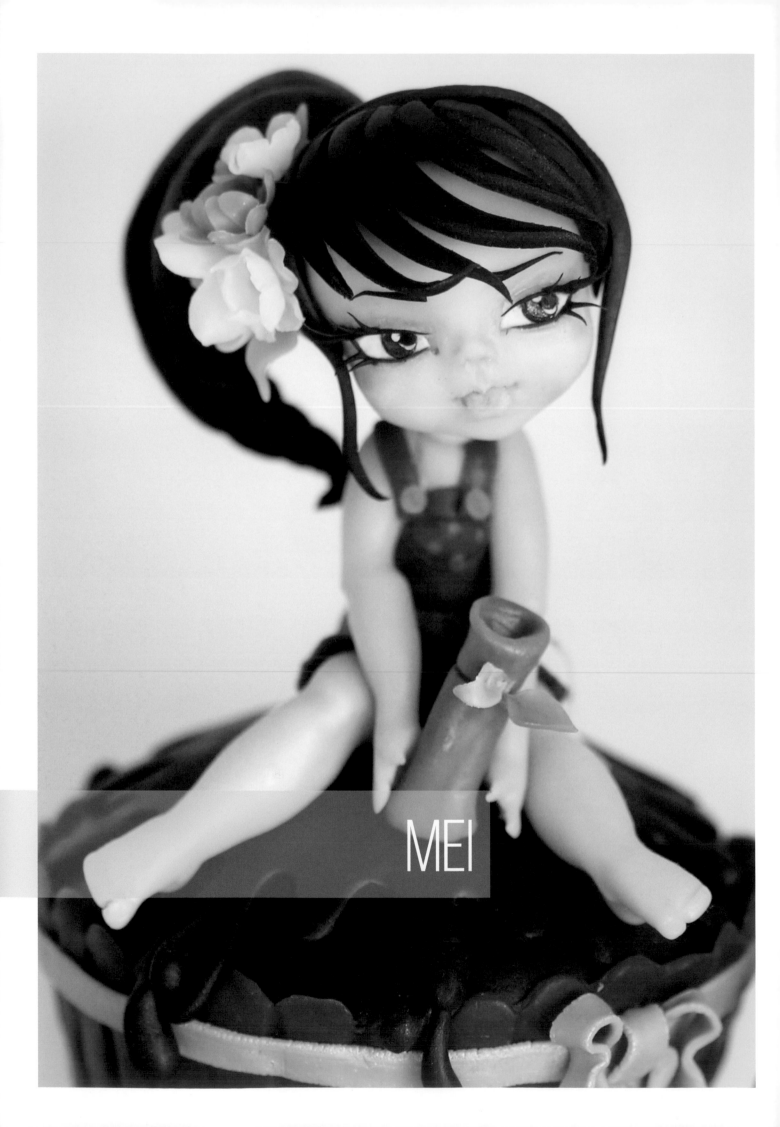

MEI

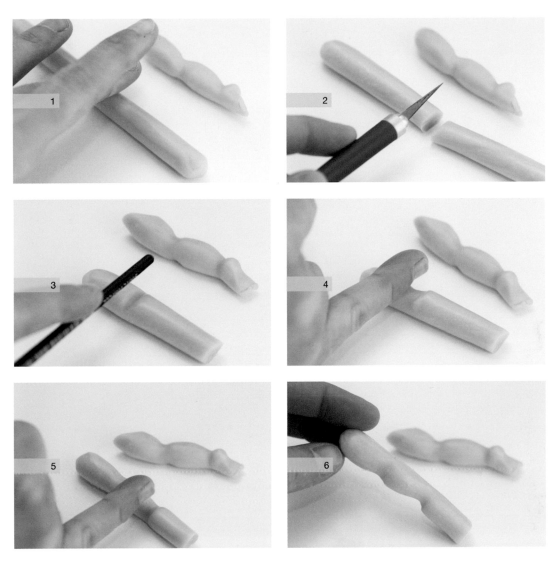

LEGS

1. Take 6 g of flesh-colored modeling chocolate. Roll into sausage shape.
2. Cut into two equal lengths.
3. About 2 cm from one end, press in the side of your brush and rotate 180°.
4. Smooth out with your finger.
5. Shape and narrow the angle.
6. You should end up with this shape, one side of which is smooth and the other curved in.

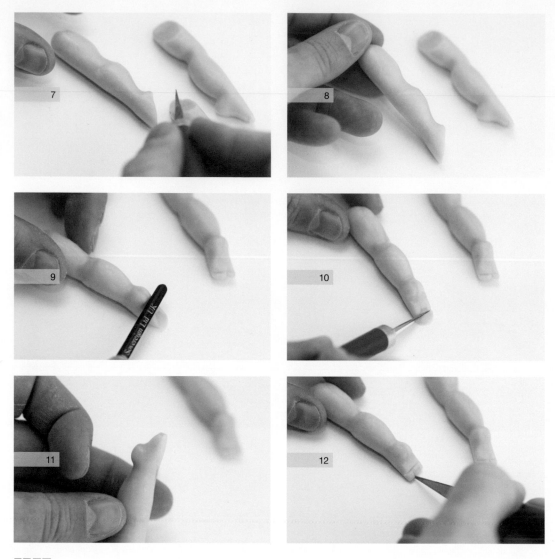

FEET

7. Position the leg on its side, then trim diagonally to shape the foot.

8. Repeat steps 16-21 for the other leg.

9. Position the leg on the smooth side and rotate the side of your brush gently against the base of the foot to shape the heel.

10. Cut across to create the toe section.

11. The foot will look like this.

12. Draw a line 2 mm up to define the toes. Then divide it into three parts. The first will be for the big toe; the others will each be divided in two, making the other four toes.

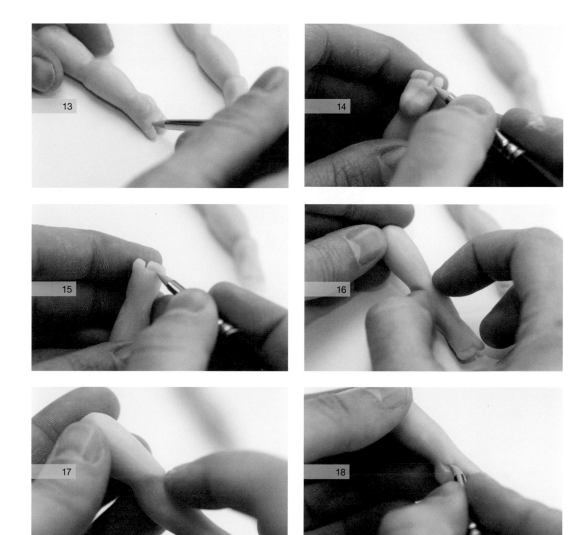

TOES AND KNEES

13. Define and shape the toes with your clay shaper.

14. Separate the big toe from the smaller toes.

15. Draw a line on the front of the foot just above the toes.

16. In the middle of the leg, pinch gently towards the front to bring out the knee.

17. Draw a U.

18. Draw a little U on each side of the foot at the ankle.

OVERALLS

19. Take 10 g of violet modeling chocolate, roll into a ball, then a sausage shape (2.5 cm in diameter).
20. Thin down two thirds of the sausage shape.
21. Cut.
22. Take 5 g of modeling chocolate and make a pear.
23. Cut it so the cut surface is the same size as the cut surface of the violet piece.
24. Join the two cut surfaces.
25. Thin the point some more and trim.
26. Place the rounded side to the back and the flatter side to the front.

27. Position the legs, trimming as necessary to keep in proportion.

28. Roll a little violet modeling chocolate very thin. Cut out two strips.

29. Wrap them around each leg and trim.

30. Smooth out the joins with your clay shaper.

31. Wrap two narrower, thicker strips around each edge.

32. Cut out a circle and apply it.

33. Trim and smooth.

34. Put a little ribbon around the waist.

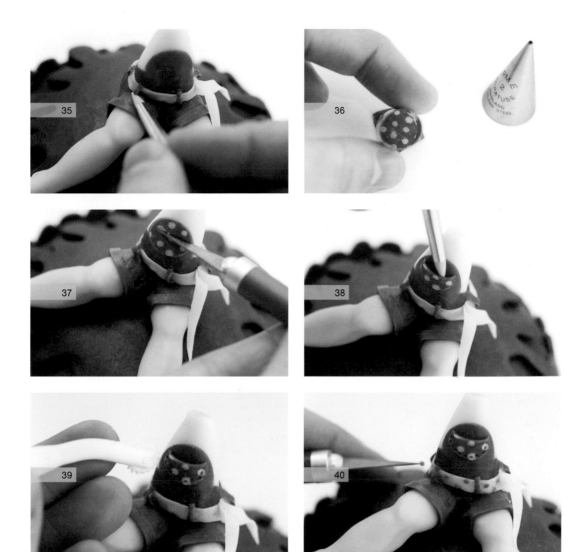

35. Then the belt loops.

36. Using pastry tube nozzle N° 2, put little white dots on a bit of the violent modeling chocolate. Smooth with your roller, then cut out a circle.

37. Put it on the front and cut at the desired length.

38. Open up the pocket.

39. Draw "stitches" around the edge.

40. Add violet dots to the belt.

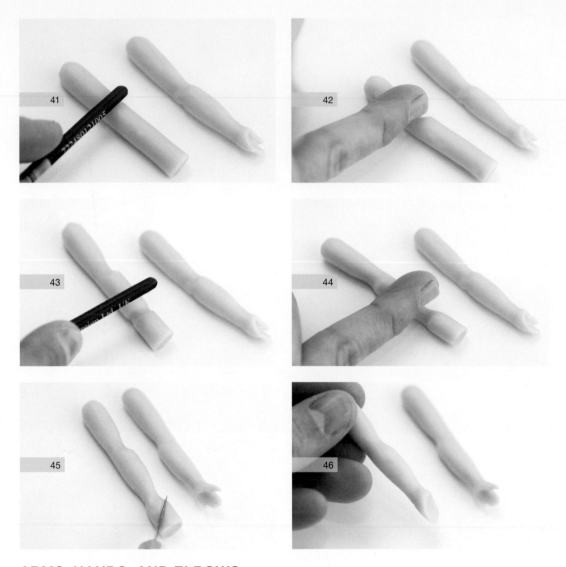

ARMS, HANDS, AND ELBOWS

41. Take 6 g of flesh-colored modeling chocolate. Roll into a sausage shape. Cut in two equal lengths.

42. About 2 cm from one end, press in the side of your brush and rotate 180°.

43. Smooth out with your finger.

44. Press in the side of your brush and rotate if 360°.

45. Shape the wrist.

46. Position the arm on its side, then trim diagonally to shape the hand.

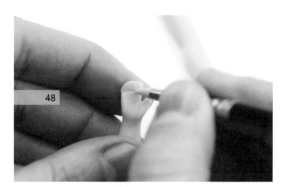

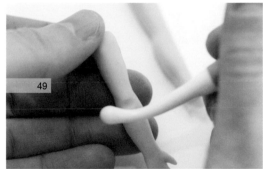

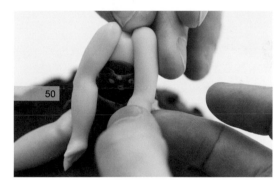

HANDS

47. Cut out a triangle to separate the thumb.

48. Draw a line.

49. On the smooth part of the arm, halfway up, press with your bone tool to bring out the elbow.

50. Position the two arms.

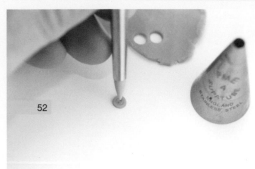

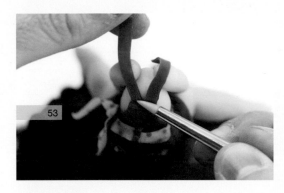

BUTTONS

51. Roll out a little green modeling chocolate and cut two circles with pastry tube nozzle N° 2; trace another circle in the middle with nozzle N° 1.

52. Draw two button holes.

53. Cut two strips and put them over the shoulders.

54. Put the buttons on the front of the overall straps.

55. Now we can concentrate on the head.

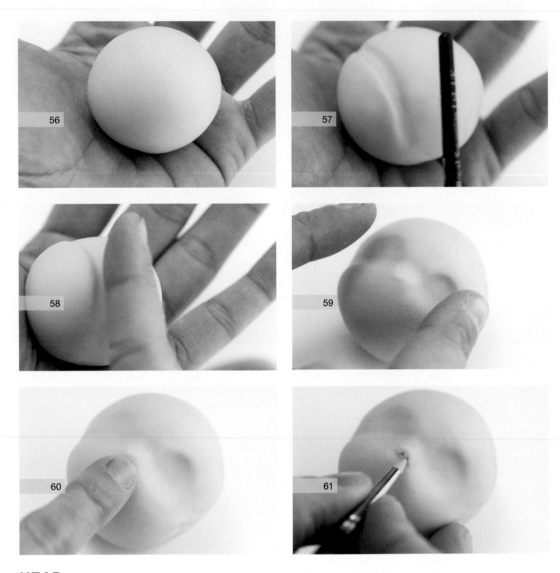

HEAD

56. Take 30 g of flesh-colored modeling chocolate and roll it into a ball.

57. Use a brush handle to trace a 180° arc.

58. Smooth out with your finger.

59. Use your index fingers symmetrically to hollow out the eye sockets.

60. Press in and up in the middle of the lower hemisphere.

61. Sculpt the nose, indicating nostril wings and openings.

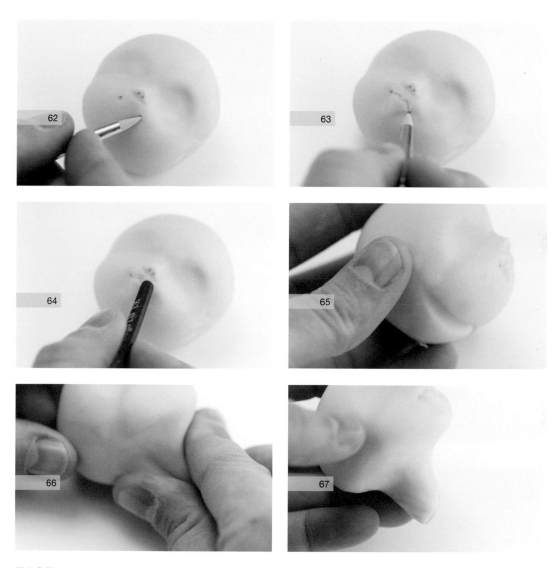

FACE

62. Mark two points 3mm away from the nose. Starting from each point, draw an oblique line. Smooth out.

63. Shape the line joining the two points.

64. Stroke the upper lip with the tip of your clay molder as though you were applying lipstick.

65. Use the brush handle to trace a 180° arc separating the jawline from the neck.

66. Pinch and push in.

67. Shape the back of the neck.

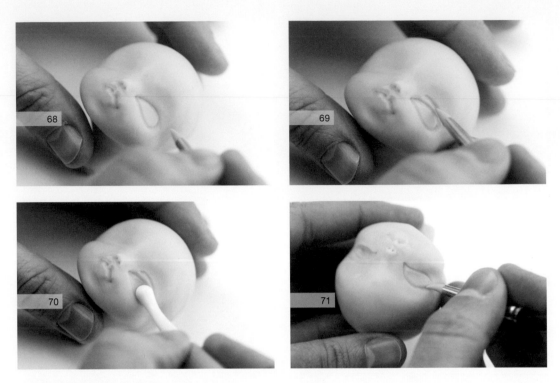

68. Draw a horizontal teardrop.
69. Add a line 1 mm above for the eyelid.
70. Deepen the interior of the teardrop shape by about 1 mm.
71. Repeat steps 68-70. To ensure optimal symmetry, turn the head upside down.

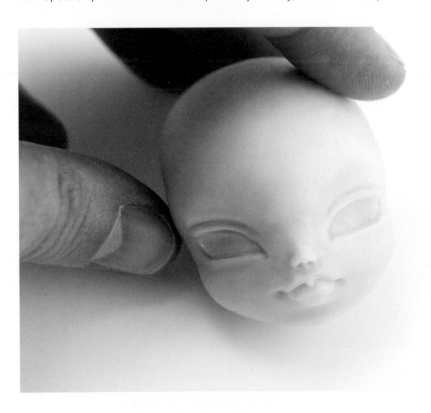

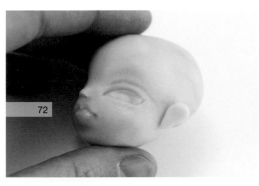

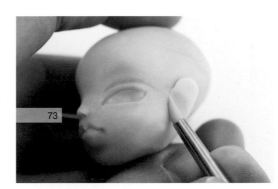

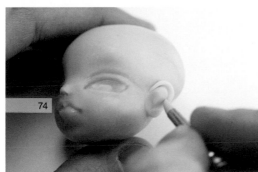

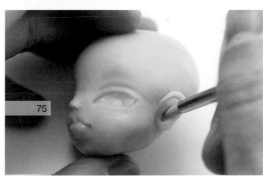

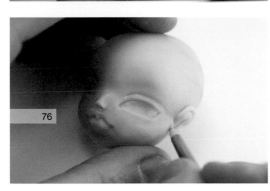

EARS

72. Cut out a little teardrop shape in line with the corner of the eye.

73. Smooth out joins.

74. Draw a line (the helix) on the outer edge of the ear.

75. Use your brush to hollow out the earhole.

76. Sculpt the tragus. Repeat for the other ear.

EYES

77. Dilute the ivory color (Wilton Gel) in a little water; paint all features.

78. Dust a little peach colored powder (Rainbow Dust) on lips and cheeks.

79. Place a little red on the tear ducts.

80. For the eyes, we will need pastry tube nozzles N° 0, 1.5, 2.5, and 4, as well as a mini teardrop cutter.

81. Cut out two teardrop shapes, position them, and trim.

82. With nozzle N° 4, cut out two black circles and two green circles for the iris.

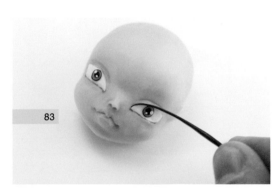

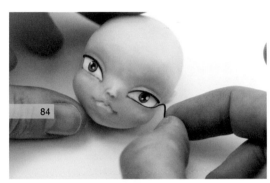

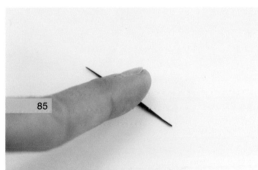

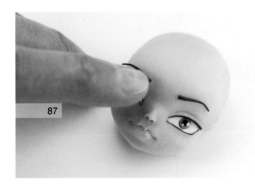

83. Roll out a very fine black thread.

84. Position it all around the eye. Do the same for the other eye.

85. Repeat step 99.

86. Cut in two.

87. Position the eyebrows.

HAIR

88. Roll out black modeling chocolate 2mm thick; cut out a circle of the same diameter as the head. Put it on top of her head.

89. Cut out another, smaller circle. Cut this circle into slices with the same cutter.

90. Assemble.

91. Position her bangs.

92. Roll three pointed cones of the same size. Join their bases, then their points.

93. Twist.

94. Position her ponytail.

95

96

97

98

99

95. Roll five tiny eyelashes (of diminishing size).

96. Put three lashes on top and two on the bottom.

97. Almost there!

98. Position a wooden stick and cut.

99. Set the head in place.

ACCESSORIES

100. Roll out white and green modeling chocolate very thin (less than 1 mm). Cut out flowers and leaves.

101. Put each flower on a sponge; press from the outside of the petals in, so the flower closes.

102. Press into the center to close the flower up.

103. Position the flowers and leaves on the side of the head, above the ponytail.

EUROPE

SHEEP

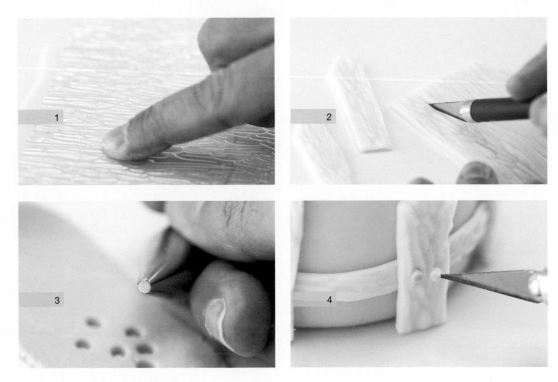

FENCE DECORATIONS

1. Roll out white modeling chocolate. Use a wood grain texture sheet.

2. Cut out horizontal bars and vertical boards.

3. Use a round-tipped nozzle to cut out nails.

4. Position the fence all around the cake.

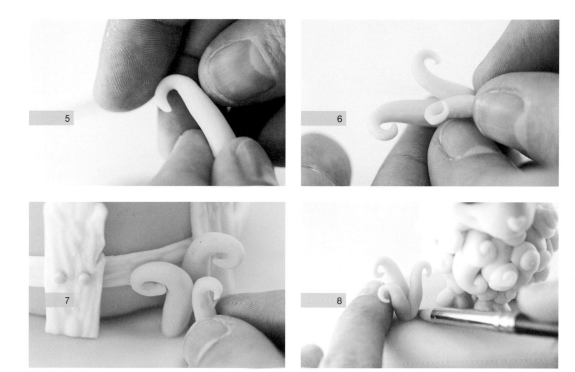

GRASS DECORATIONS

5. Roll green 'carrot' shapes and twist their points.

6. Make little tufts, putting two or three 'blades' together.

7. Position them around the fence.

8. Add a few tufts of grass to the top of the cake.

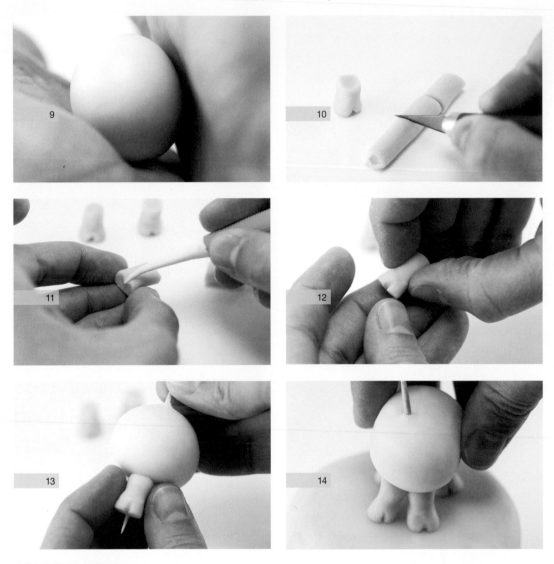

SHEEP'S BODY

9. Roll a ball and flatten it slightly to make an egg.

10. Make a flesh-colored sausage shape; cut it into four legs.

11. Mark out the hoofs.

12. Narrow the upper end of the leg.

13. Stick a toothpick at a slant through the body towards the front legs; leave a bit sticking out to hold the head.

14. Add the back legs and place on the cake.

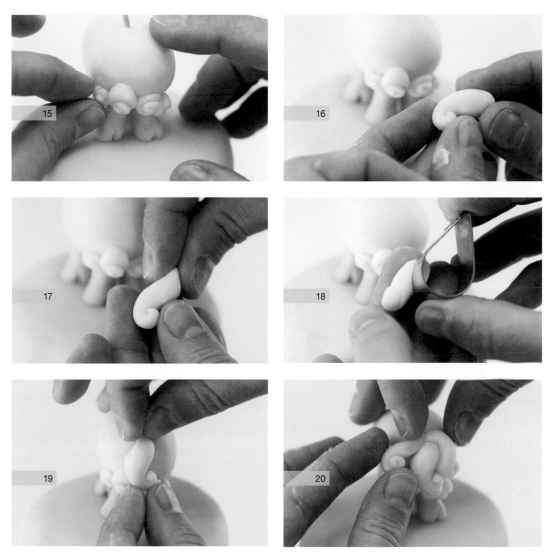

WOOL

15. Roll several sizes of 'snail' shapes and arrange around the legs.

16. Make some 'carrot' shapes and twist the point a third of the way down.

17. Pinch the other end.

18. Cut out a piece of the base.

19. Position under the neck and the body.

20. Repeat, alternating snail and carrot shapes, all over the body.

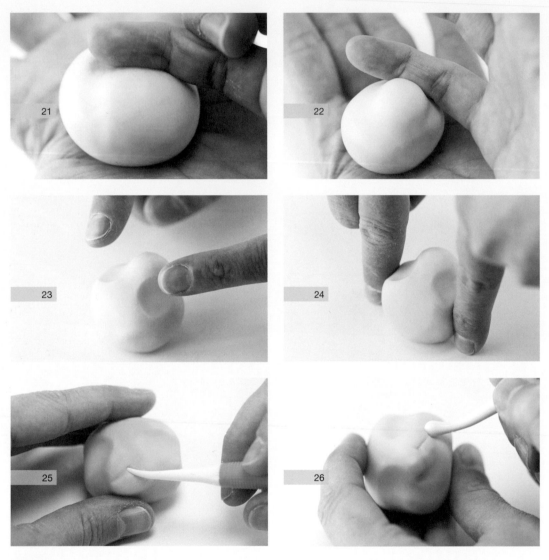

HEAD

21. Roll a ball and, using your ring finger, mold a rounded shape for the muzzle.
22. Narrow the muzzle.
23. Hollow out the eye sockets.
24. Mold the temples.
25. Shape the mouth with the imprint tool.
26. Shape the dimples with the small bone modeling tool.

EYES

27. Cut out two large dark brown teardrops, two smaller white teardrops, two even smaller brown circles for the retina, and two blue crescents for the iris.

28. Take the two large dark brown teardrops and cut out 1mm from the edge.

29. Position the white first, then put the retina and the iris together like a puzzle and position them. Position the eyelash, trimming the outer edge.

30. Fold the eyelash on the inner edge.

31. Cut three dots with the pastry tube nozzles. Put two on top and two on the bottom.

32. Add white highlights to give the eyes sparkle.

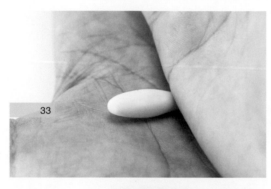

WOOL

33. As you did for the body, make carrot and snail shapes.

34. Curl the ends.

35. First position the slightly twisted carrots.

36. Then the snails.

37. Give them movement.

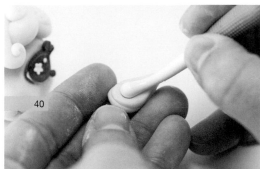

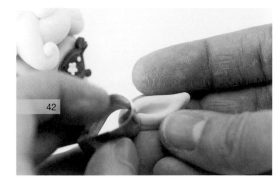

EARS

38. Cut out two flesh-colored teardrop shapes, then two larger white ones.
39. Place one on top of the other.
40. Use the bone modeling tool to hollow out the ears.
41. Fold and pinch the ear, twisting the point slightly.
42. Cut out a little of the base to fit the curve of the head.
43. Position the ears on the head.

NOSE AND ACCESSORIES

44. Cut out a mini-heart and position it on the muzzle.

45. And now at last you can put the pretty little head on its body.

46. Why not add some flowers to make it even fancier?

OCEANIA

KOALA

CUPCAKE DECORATIONS

1. Roll out white modeling chocolate for your cupcake.
2. Cut a rectangle the size of the cup.
3. Make dots in different colors.
4. Position the first column of dots, then the second, varying colors.
5. Smooth out with your rolling pin.
6. Wrap around the cake.

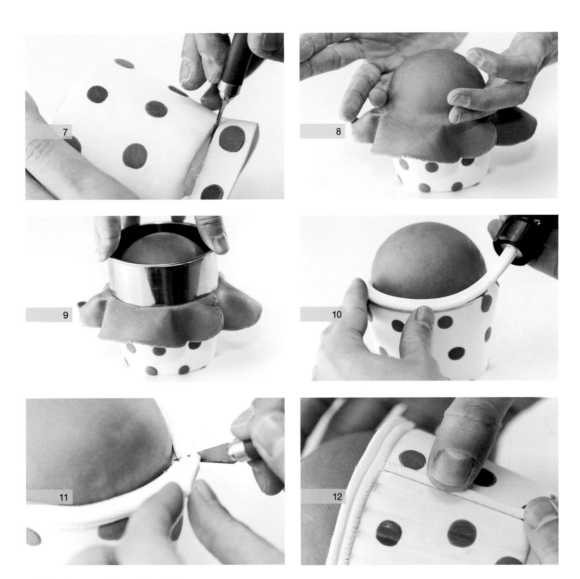

7. Trim the modeling chocolate.

8. Make a hemisphere out of cake. Roll out pink modeling chocolate; cover the cupcake dome.

9. Trim.

10. With your sugar gun, run a ribbon around the edge of the cup.

11. Cut and join the two cut surfaces.

12. Take a little stick and indent the cup surface every 5 mm.

13. Roll out brown modeling chocolate and cut a big circle.

14. Make 'drips' all around the edge.

15. Position it on the dome.

16. Smooth the edges with your small bone modeling tool.

17. Roll a sausage shape and put it on top, winding it around like a swirl of whipped cream.

18. Cut out a few little flowers and put them on the 'whipped cream'. Add edible sparkles for flair.

BON BON DECORATIONS

19. Roll some little pink bulb shapes and thin strips of white.

20. Wrap around the bulbs in peppermint twist style.

21. Arrange on cupcake.

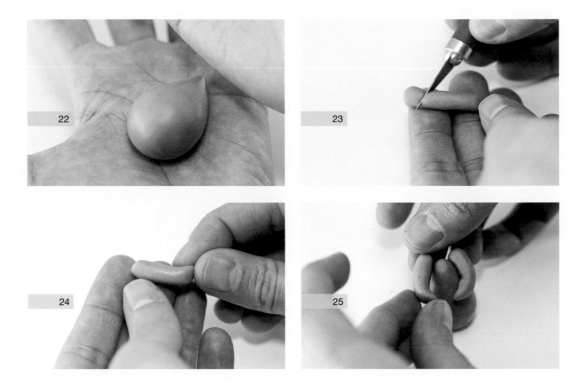

KOALA'S BODY

22. Make a pear for the body.

23. Roll a sausage shape and cut one end on a slant, the other straight.

24. Round off the straight end and bend the slanted end.

25. Position the arms.

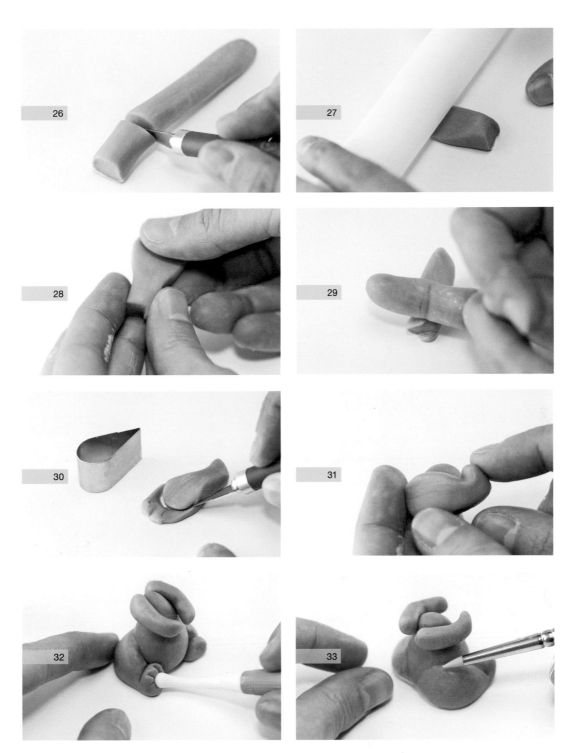

26. Roll a sausage shape and cut it in two.

27. Flatten one end.

28. Pinch.

29. Roll the front part using your ring finger.

30. Use a teardrop cutter to shape the rounded end, finishing it off with a scalpel.

31. Bend the front part to bring out the foot.

32. Position the legs. Make three lines on each paw and use the small bone modeling tool to hollow the sole of the foot.

33. Smooth out the joins.

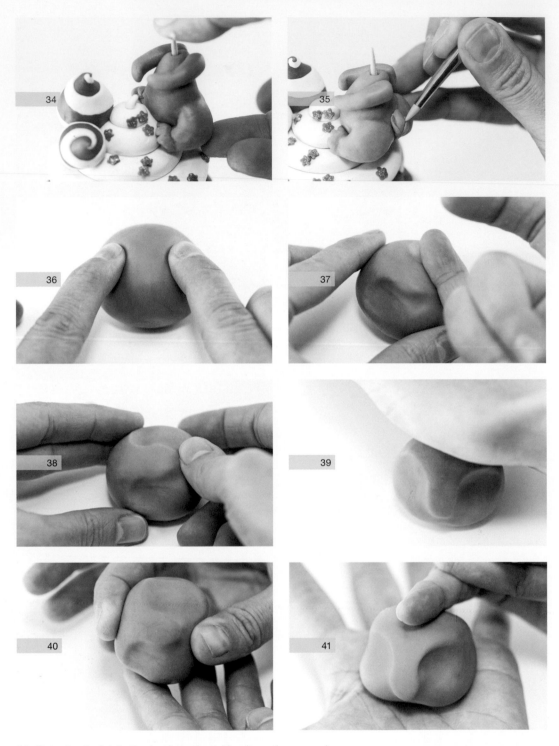

34. Put a toothpick in the body and position it on the cupcake.

35. Add a little tail. Mark the creases.

HEAD

36. Make a ball and shape the eye sockets.

37. Using your ring finger, press on the inner corners of the eyes to bring out the muzzle.

38. Round off the lower jaw.

39. Flatten the head slightly.

40. Sculpt the cheeks with your thumb.

41. Shape the top of the head with your ring finger.

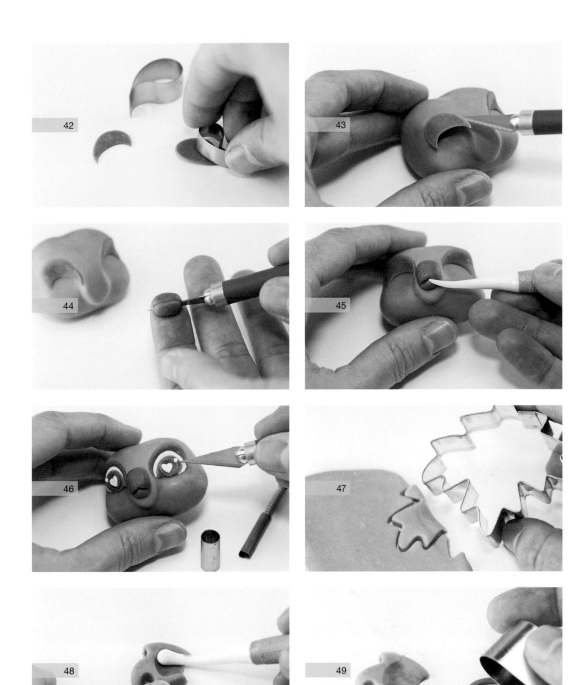

EYES, NOSE, AND EARS

42. Cut two crescents.
43. Put them on the brow bones.
44. Roll a little lozenge. Cut it in two.
45. Position it as the nose. Draw the mouth as an upside-down V.
46. Position the pupil, iris, and heart-shaped highlights.
47. Use a cutter in the shape of a maple leaf to cut out the ears.
48. Use your small bone modeling tool to hollow out the middle.
49. Add a bit of pink.

50. Cut the base on a curve.

51. Position the ears on the head and smooth out the joins. Don't forget to add the nostrils.

ACCESSORIES AND COOKIE

52. Put a little bonbon in his hands.

53. Set the head in place.

54. Give her a little bow! Cut out two hearts and join their points.

ACKNOWLEDGMENTS

A heartfelt helping of love, sweetness, and tenderness for my two sunbeams, Tatiana and Yelena. They reawakened my artistic instincts and creativity, and without them, these passions would have been left in the lost world of childhood memories.

To my companion, Gil, who gave me my most precious treasures, who shared his enthusiasms and brought me into the digital age.

To my spiritual sister, Bea, who was always there to hear me and encourage me, whatever the circumstance.

To Isabelle, personal coach, who brought her insight and dynamism to bear on my anxieties, letting me bring ChokoLate to you.

To my family, near and far, who supported me regardless of distance.

Thanks to all my friends, to everyone who follows and encourages me, near or far, whether every day or now and then.

And You, dear readers, fans of my ChokoLate page, without whom this book would have no meaning, since it was created for you.

United States	Pastry Portal www.pastryportal.com
	Global Sugar Art www.globalsugarart.com
	Swank Cake Design www.swankcakedesign.com'
	Country Kitchen Sweet Art www.countrykitchensa.com
The Netherlands	De Leukste Taarten www.deleukstetaartenshop.nl
United Kingdom	Squires Kitchen www.squires-shop.com
	Cakes Cookies and Crafts www.cakescookiesandcraftsshop.co.uk
	Lakeland www.lakeland.co.uk
Australia	Cake Decorating Central www.cakedecoratingcentral.com.au
	BakeBoss www.bakeboss.com.au
New Zealand	Kiwi Cake Supplies www.kiwicakes.co.nz
	Cake Stuff www.cakestuff.co.nz